Alfred's Premier Piano Course

Dennis Alexander • Gayle Kowalchyk • E. L. Lancaster • Victoria McArthur • Martha Mier

Alfred's *Premier Piano Course* Pop and Movie Hits Book 3 includes familiar pieces that reinforce concepts included in Lesson Book 3. The music continues the strong pedagogical focus of the course while providing the enjoyment of playing familiar popular music.

The pieces in this book correlate page-by-page with the materials in Lesson Book 3. They should be assigned according to the instructions in the upper right corner of each page of this book. They also may be assigned as review material at any time after the student has passed the designated Lesson Book page. Pop and Movie Hits 3 also can be used to supplement any beginning piano method.

Allowing students to study music they enjoy is highly motivating. Consequently, reading and rhythm skills often improve greatly when studying pop and movie music. The authors hope that the music in Pop and Movie Hits 3 brings hours of enjoyment.

Edited by Morton Manus

Produced by
Alfred Music
P.O. Box 10003
Van Nuys, CA 91410-0003
alfred.com

Printed in USA.

ISBN-10: 0-7390-7405-9

ISBN-13: 978-0-7390-7405-3

CONTENTS

Use with Alfred's Premier Piano Course
Lesson Book 3, pages 4–5

California, Here I Come

Words and Music by
Al Jolson, Bud DeSylva and Joseph Meyer

Cal - i - for - nia, here I come,

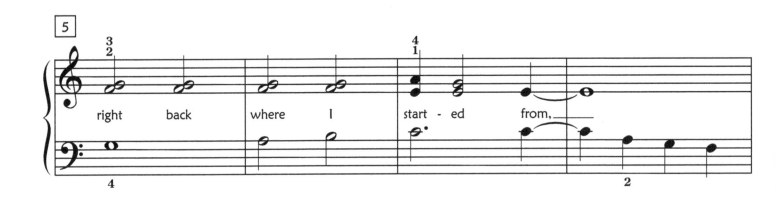

right back where I start - ed from,

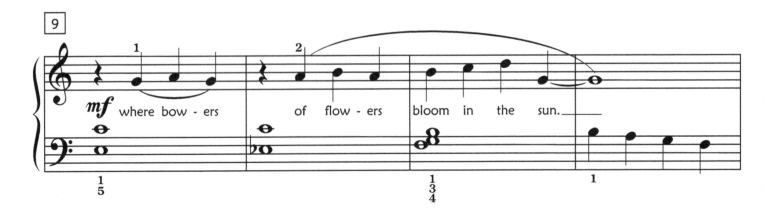

where bow - ers of flow - ers bloom in the sun.

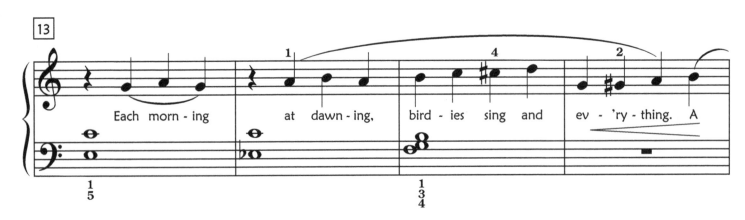

Each morn - ing at dawn - ing, bird - ies sing and ev - 'ry - thing. A

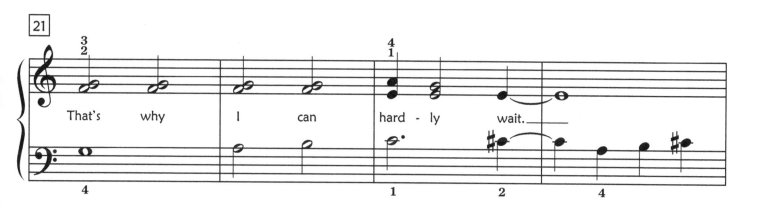

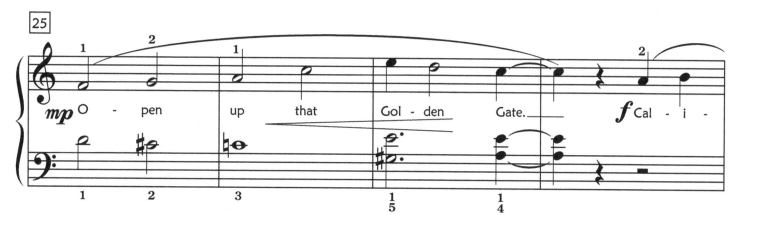

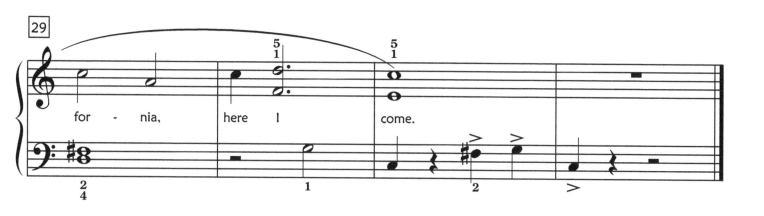

Splish Splash

Words and Music by
Bobby Darin and Jean Murray

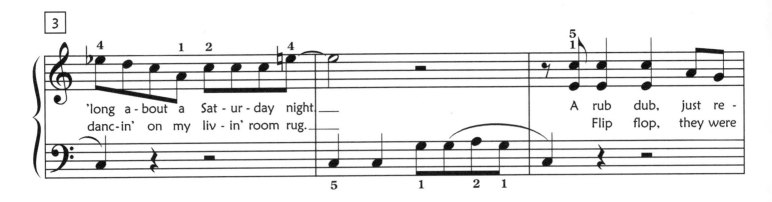

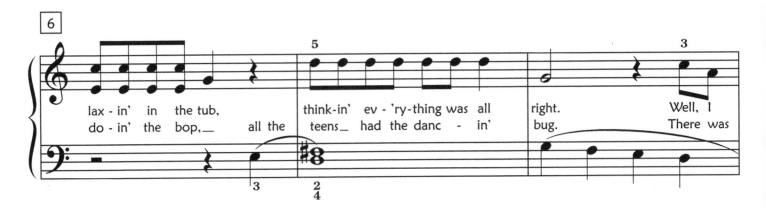

Bridge Over Troubled Water

Words and Music by
Paul Simon

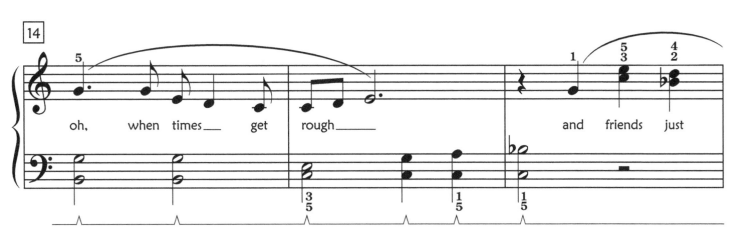

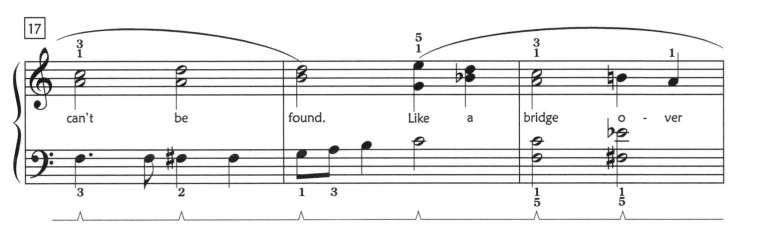

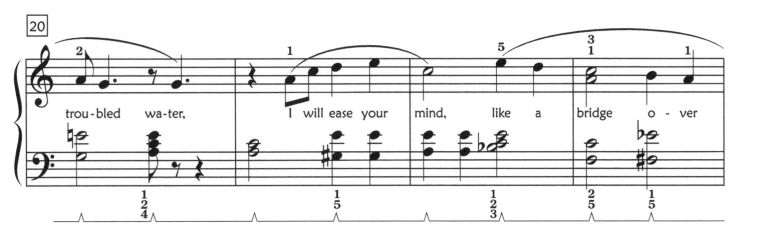

Raindrops Keep Fallin' on My Head

(from *Butch Cassidy and the Sundance Kid*)

Words by Hal David
Music by Burt Bacharach

Looking Back
(Love Theme from *Glee*)

Music by Kerry Muzzey

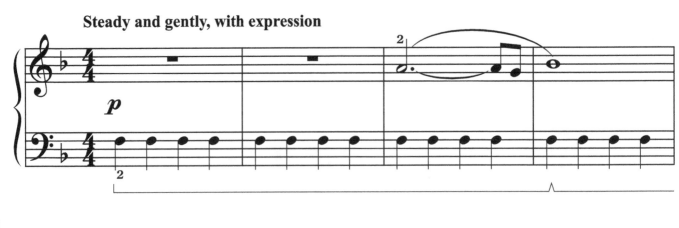

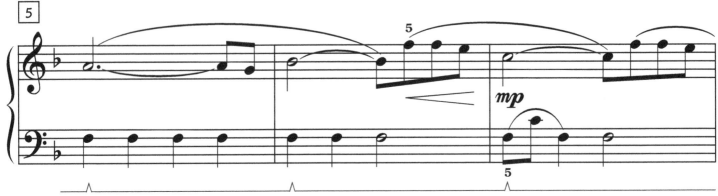

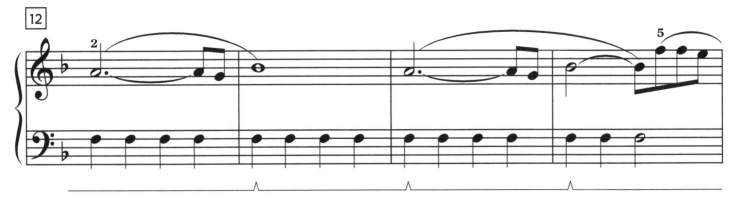

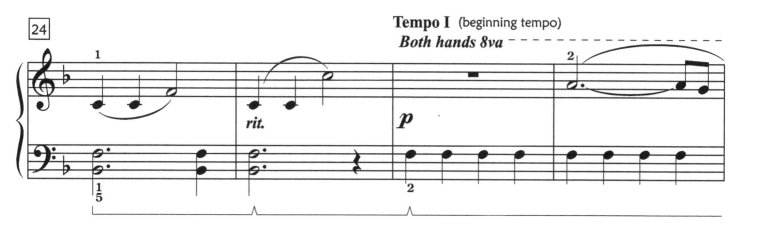

Someday My Prince Will Come

Words by Larry Morey
Music by Frank Churchill

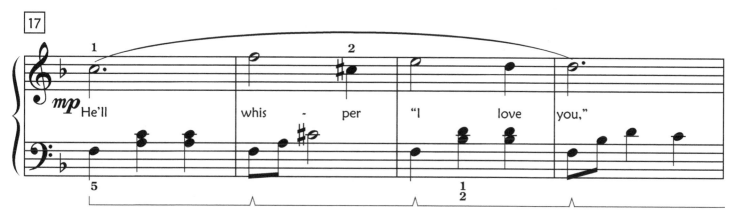

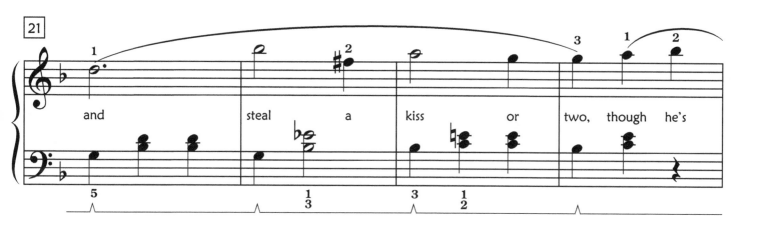

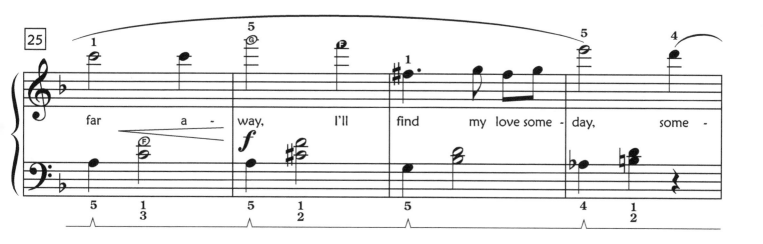

14

Wipe Out

By The Surfaris

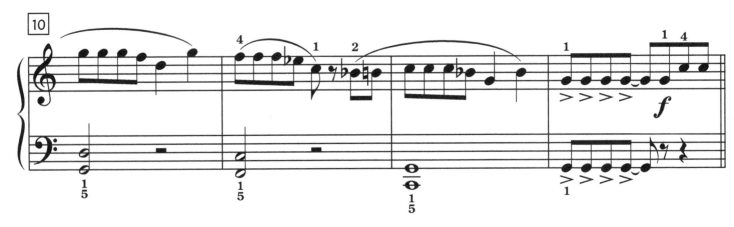

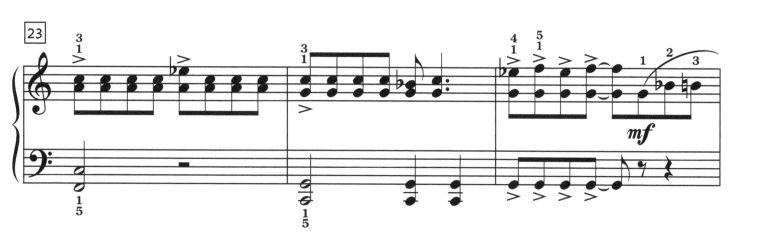

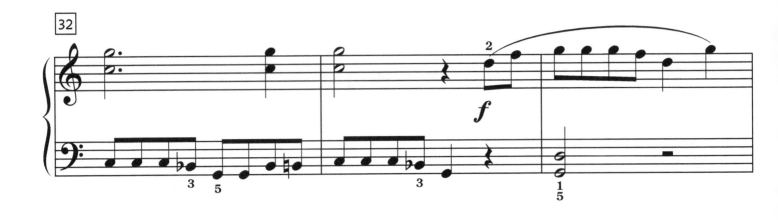

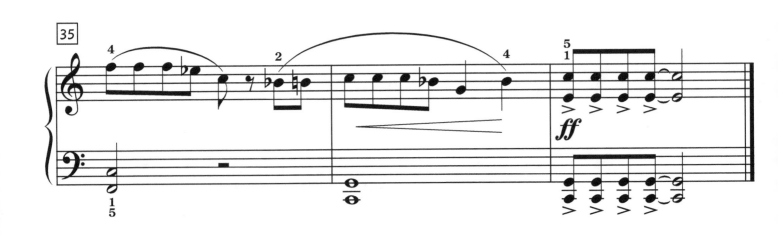

Breakaway

Words and Music by
Matthew Gerrard, Bridget Benenate and Avril Lavigne

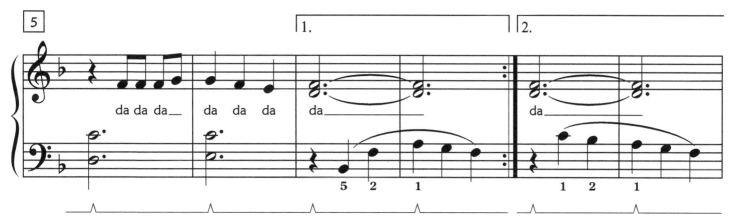

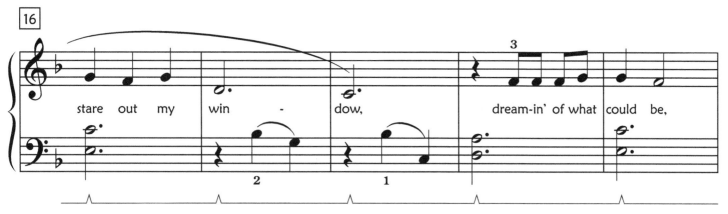

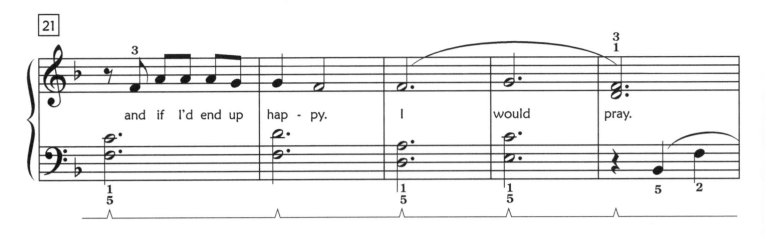

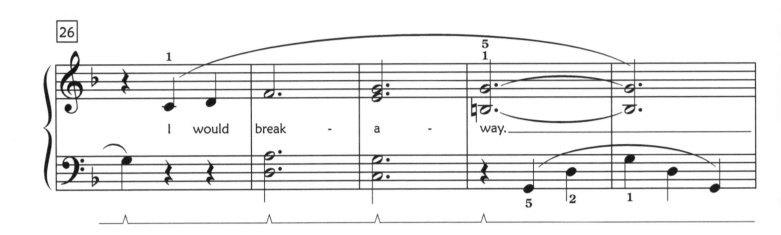

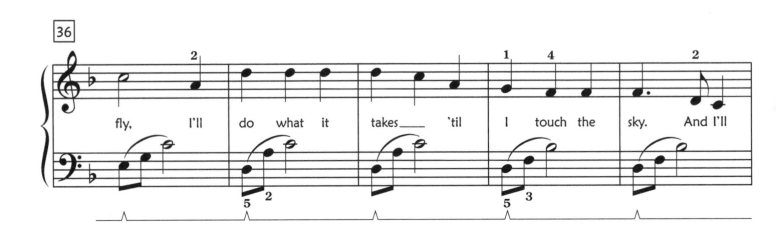

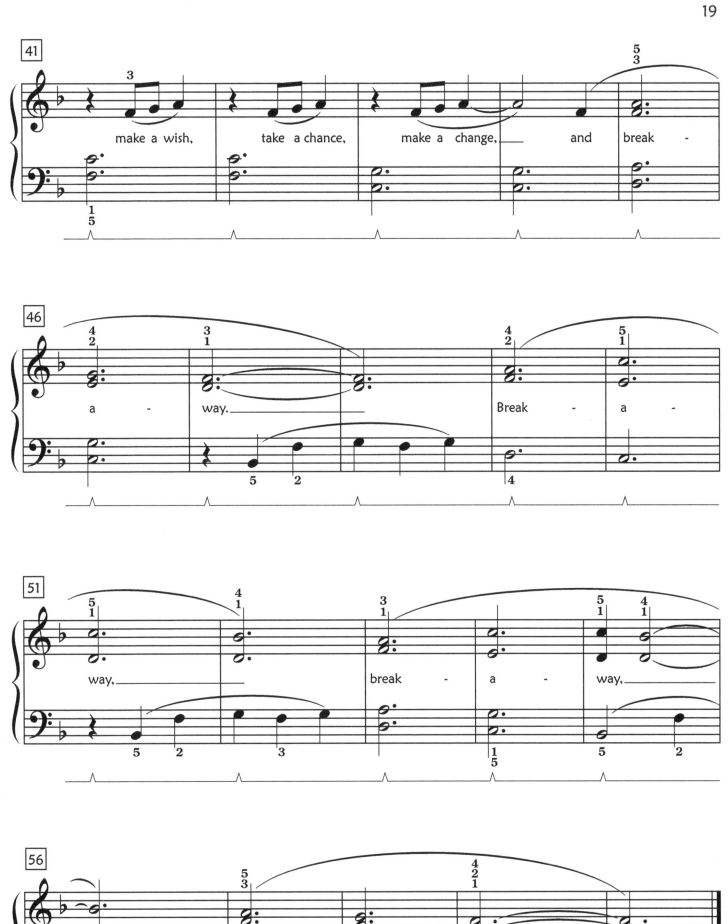

Somewhere My Love (Lara's Theme)

(from *Dr. Zhivago*)

Music by Maurice Jarre
Lyric by Paul Francis Webster

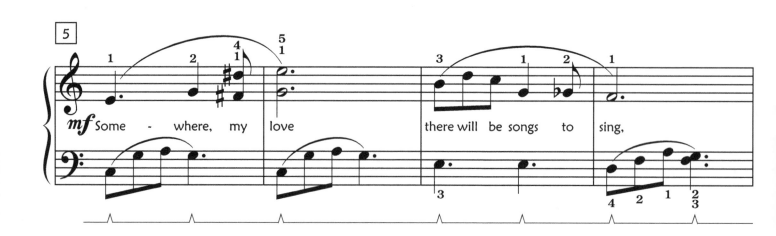

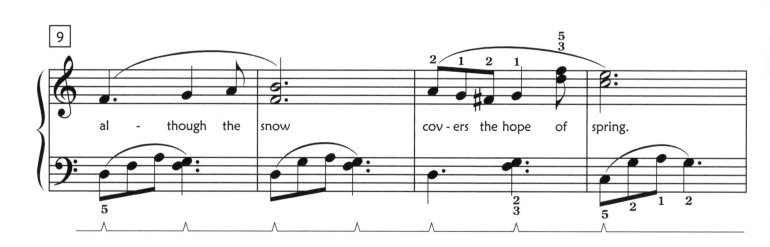

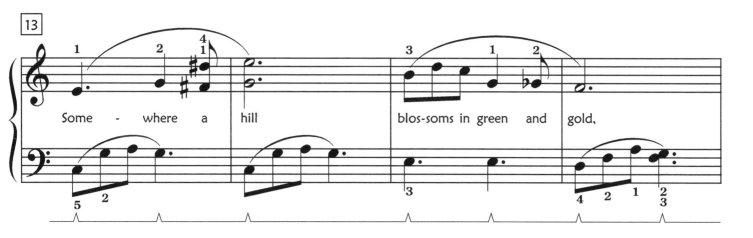

13

Some - where a hill blos-soms in green and gold,

17

and there are dreams, all that your heart can hold.

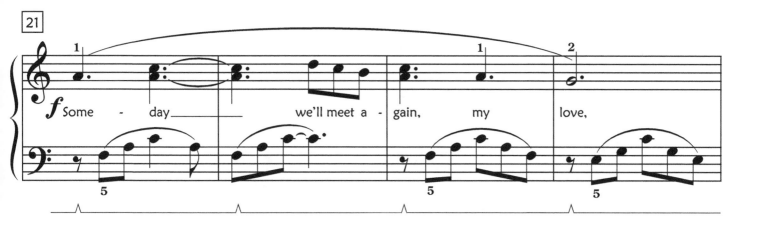

21

f Some - day_____ we'll meet a - gain, my love,

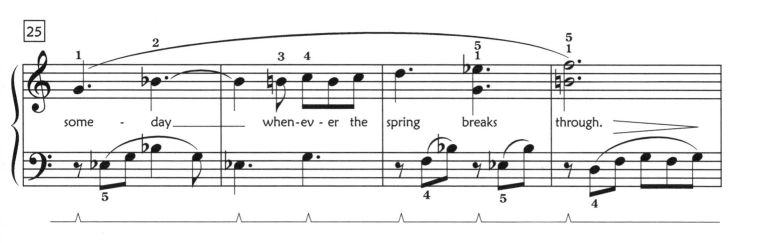

25

some - day_____ when-ev - er the spring breaks through.

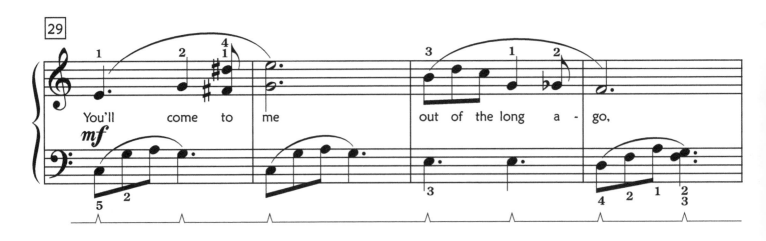

Don't Stop Believin'

Words and Music by
Jonathan Cain, Neal Schon and Steve Perry

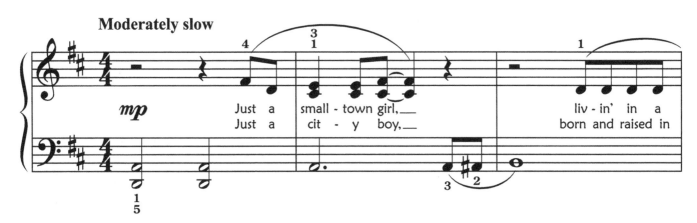

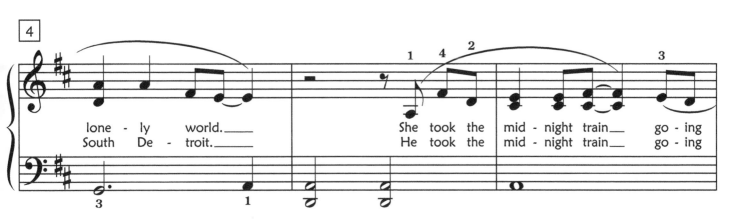

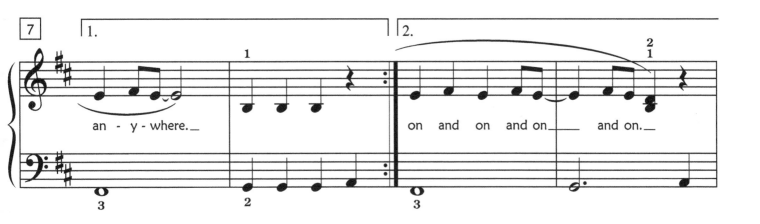

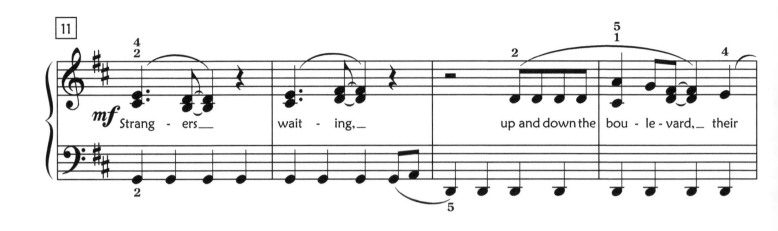

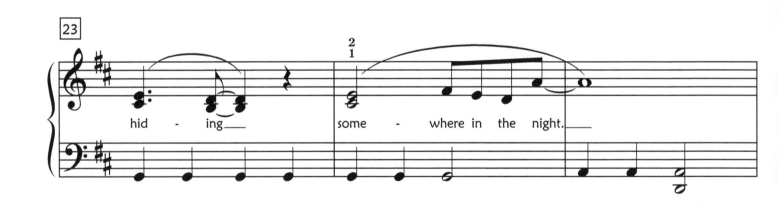

Colors of the Wind

(from Walt Disney's *Pocahontas*)

Lyrics by Stephen Schwartz
Music by Alan Menken

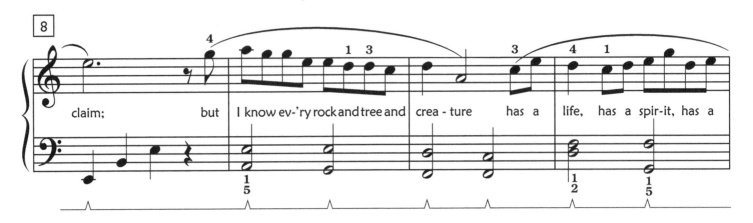

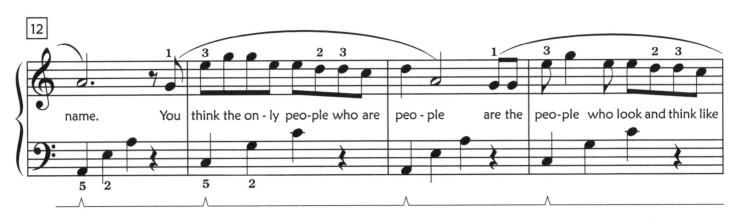

Baby

Words and Music by
Terius Nash, Christopher Stewart, Christine Flores,
Christopher Bridges and Justin Bieber

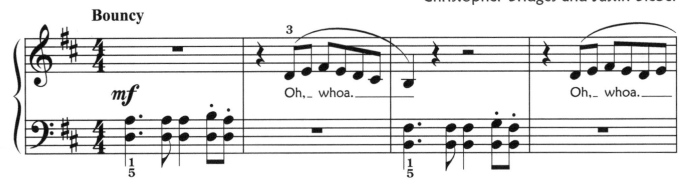

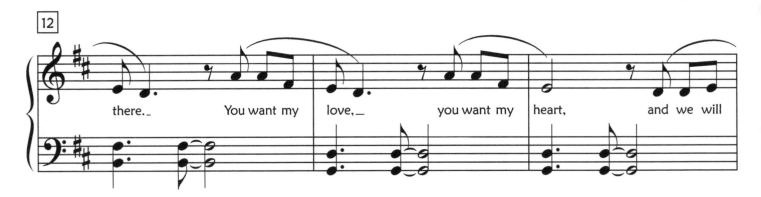

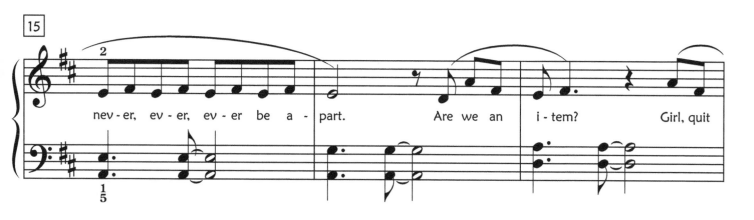

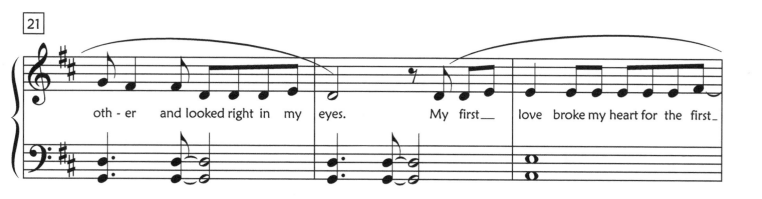

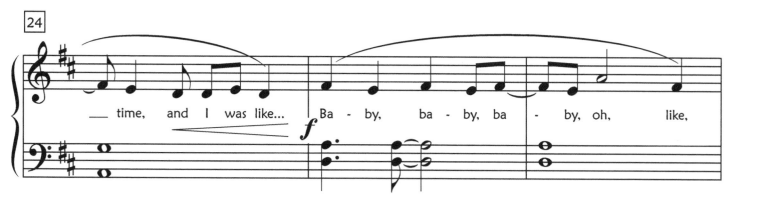

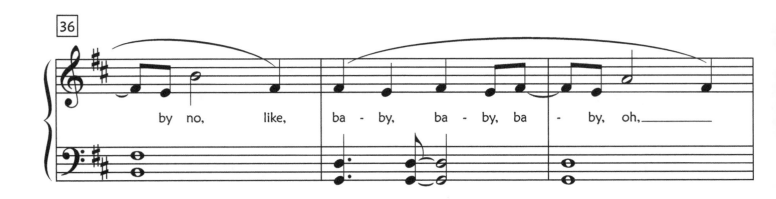

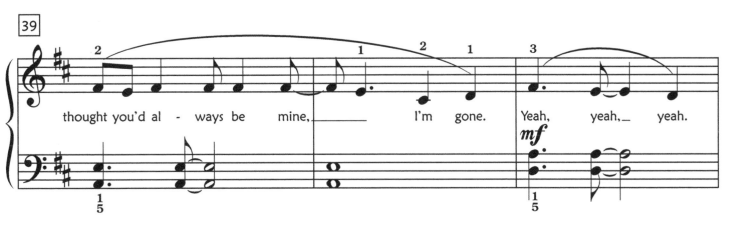

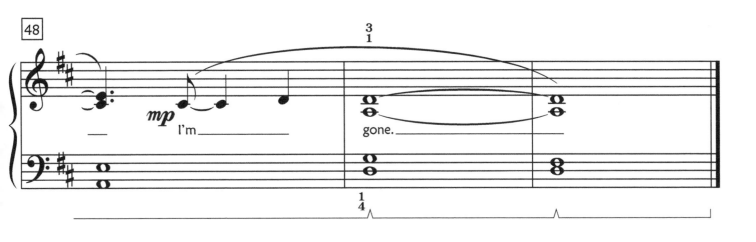